"Please Help Me, God"

Sr. Mary Rose McGeady

Covenant House

DEDICATED
to the 400,000 children
we have had the privilege of serving
these past 25 years — kids who were
scared, cold, hungry, alone and most of all,
desperate to find someone who cared.
We are honored to have helped.

Table of Contents

Introduction

"Their scribbled notes to God...."

If you were to sit quietly in the back of our chapel at Covenant House you might notice a couple of things.

First, you'd notice that our chapel is one of the few peaceful places at Covenant House. As the largest crisis shelter for homeless kids on this continent, Covenant House is a pretty crazy place. We serve 1,200 children a night — kids from all walks of life and from every part of the country. On most nights there is noise, lots of noise that comes from lots of pain, lots of joy, lots of despair and lots of hope.

But if you were to sit in the chapel, you'd escape most of that.

What you would see, however, is a kid every once in a while, who would enter respectfully, walk to the front of the chapel and drop a slip of paper in a special box — our prayer box.

On these scraps of paper, my kids scribble their notes to God.

When I empty the box, I often find words of anger ("God, how could you let Dad beat me like that?"), bargaining ("Dear God, I'll go home and stay in school if you'll make Mom stay sober."), doubt ("After the hell I've been through, why should I believe in You?")

and terror ("Please, God, don't let my HIV test come back positive.").

This morning when I reached into the box, the first scrap of paper I touched held this heart-wrenching plea:

"Please Help Me, God."

I felt glued to the floor.

I am Sister Mary Rose McGeady. For seven years, my life has been wrapped up in this place. As president of Covenant House, I have met thousands of homeless kids. Somehow, everything I believe about these kids, everything I have come to love and respect about them was summed up in that four-word plea.

"Please Help Me, God."

I don't know which one of our kids wrote this note, if it was a boy or a girl, or someone who's stayed in our shelter a day or a month. But in a way, I know *exactly* who this kid is. It's a kid we see hundreds of times every day here in our shelter.

Every day I meet hundreds of kids who've endured every imaginable horror (and some you can't even imagine) in their homes and on the streets. Their lives are one story after another of abuse, degradation and abandonment.

And so, after all that, they wonder if anyone really knows they are hurting, or cares.

"Please Help Me, God."

They come to us exhausted, hungry, cold, desperate — without any of the basics of life that every child has a right to expect. It's not hard to understand why they would cry out this plea. In a world — their own unique heartbreaking world — that is agonizing, painful and terrifying, these kids need something, anything, to cling to and believe in.

"Please Help Me, God."

And so, they reach out as best they can. Some of the most moving experiences of my life have been listening to these special pleas, as part of our prayer circles. Unless you have been there yourself, it's almost impossible to comprehend how moving those moments are, to hear kids read the scripture and pray from their hearts to the God who remains their friend when they have been able to rely on few others. In those moments, which I will always treasure, I can almost hear their broken hearts being repaired and soothed as they pray.

"Please Help Me, God."

We believe Covenant House is the answer to this plea, and the answer to those prayers. We are the physical embodiment of God, His hands, His heart, His eyes, His mouth. In everything we do, 24 hours a day, and 365 days a year, we love the kids as God loves them — unconditionally and with absolute respect. In many respects, our mission can be summed up in one simple and very profound commitment: We care for these kids as God cares for them.

This year, 44,000 abused or neglected kids will take refuge at our Covenant House shelters in cities all across America — in New York, Los Angeles, Ft. Lauderdale, New Orleans, Anchorage, Newark, Washington, D.C., Orlando, Atlantic City, Houston and our newest Covenant House in Detroit. And as you read this, we are also saving kids in shelters throughout Central America, as well as in Toronto (and soon, we pray, Vancouver).

As president of an organization that spends more to help homeless kids than the federal government, I've met with the President, testified before Congress and been appointed to a few commissions. When I get those opportunities, I speak for the kids. I think it is so very, very important because they have few opportunities to speak for themselves. The stories in this book are about these kids, their tragedies and their triumphs.

I have to warn you that these are not pretty stories. They are often graphic, often wrenching ... and always true ... tales of their lives.

I hope that when you've read them, you'll love and respect these kids as much as I do. And I hope you'll want to help them.

Your support can help give them hot meals, a safe place to sleep, medical care, counseling and, most of all, love.

That love, the love you and I are called to give, is the way that God proves that He reads those prayers they write on scraps of paper.

And that His kids are always loved ... and already forgiven. They are finally home.

> Sister Mary Rose McGeady
> June 9, 1997

No stranger I, to death.
He lives with me each day.
He tempts me with my grave,
and hides the price I'll pay.

A poem from
a street kid

*"The love of God
is creative to infinity."*

St. Vincent de Paul

Chapter 1

"She ... she does stuff to make money," she said.
"You know, stuff with guys she meets."

"We never knew where we were going to sleep," she said.

"Sometimes we slept in someone else's house. Sometimes we slept under some stairway. One night, our house was a big cardboard box, and my mother let me snuggle with her.

"That was a really nice night," she said wistfully.

Teresa looked up at me from her hospital bed, and tried to manage a smile. Even with her beautiful smile it was hard not to see the mass of bruises that covered her body from head to toe. She was so swollen around her mouth and eyes that she could barely breathe. I know she wanted to cry, but she wouldn't allow herself. It hurt too much to do it.

Teresa was 12 years old.

"I'm really glad you called us," I said. "I'm so sorry that you've been hurt like this," I said.

"I didn't know who else to call," she said. It was clear from the emptiness in her eyes and her voice that she really meant what she said. There *wasn't* anyone else in the world she could call.

"Do you want to tell me what happened?"

"I was visiting a friend's house, and it started to get late," she said. "I had promised my mother I would meet her at 11:00 under a bridge. That's where we've been sleeping. But before I could get there ... it ... it happened."

"It" was something I'm seeing in epidemic proportions these past few months. A guy spots a young girl alone on the streets. He jumps her and drags her to an alley, where the girl is beaten and raped. The girl screams for help, but none comes.

Only 12 years old, the girl finds herself in a dark alleyway, unconscious, bleeding, dying inside and out.

"When I woke up I ... I just kinda crawled to a phone. I had heard about your nine number, so I called that."

"Our NINELINE?" I asked. "1-800-999-9999?" This year we'll get more than 1,000,000 calls on our NINELINE, many from kids like Teresa.

"Yuh, so I dialed it. I just kept pushing nines. A lady answered on the other side. I told her where I was. Then I guess I just blanked out. I don't remember what happened after that."

When our outreach van reached Teresa she was stretched out on the pavement. She had a broken jaw, a severe concussion, contusions all across her body and three broken ribs.

We rushed her to the nearest hospital, and then worried and prayed about her all night. As soon as she woke up, I rushed to her side. I absolutely needed to be with her. I had to be there....

"Did they find my mother yet?" she asked. "She's probably under the bridge, really worried about me."

"The authorities are looking," I said. "They've spent the last 36 hours, ever since you got here, searching for her. But she hasn't turned up yet. Do you know where else she might be?"

Teresa looked away, staring at the wall, wondering what to say. "Sometimes she goes away for a while," she said. "She has to. It's part of her job."

"What does she do," I said (knowing the answer).

"She ... she does stuff to make money," she said looking down at the sheets. "You know, stuff with guys she meets." She swallowed hard while she choked out the words.

"It's not that bad when she's around. But sometimes she has to leave town to do her job."

"Has she ever left you for a long time?"

"No," Teresa said. "Never. I think the longest she was ever gone was about 17 days. But she came back."

I tried to imagine the sheer terror Teresa must have felt then, being 12 years old and all alone on the street for 17 days, not knowing when or if your mother was going to 'come home.' Where *would* you go? What *would* you do?

"How did you live?"

"It was pretty tough," she said. "I found food on the street, and I would just sleep outside. It wasn't too bad," she said. The tears forming in her eyes told me otherwise.

By that time the painkiller was taking effect, making every word tougher to speak than the last. "I think I'm going to close my eyes for just a second. I'm really, really tired."

And there, in that quiet hospital room, the little 12-year-old kid with bruises covering her body, fell asleep.

I kept looking at her, for the longest time, hoping the tormented look on her little face would melt away, but it never did. I patted her hand and said a silent prayer to God, thanking God that He had given me a chance to be there, if only for a moment.

She's part of us now. *We own her,* in the sense that God has called us to own the hurts and sorrows of every kid who comes to us, no matter how long we see them, no matter how impossible their situation. That's what our covenant is all about. Bounding ourselves to desperate kids like Teresa. Making a sacred promise to be there for them. Whenever they need us. For however long.

For Teresa, our covenant called us to "be there" during the worst 48 hours of her life. To be on the other side of the phone when she called us. Be on the other side of the hospital bed when she was all alone. And yes, to be there when it comes time to find her a good home. (Please know that Teresa will never, ever be going back to the streets. Ever! I've made that covenant with God already. We will help find her a good home. You have my promise on that.)

For other kids, our covenant with them lasts a week, a month, or in the instance of our Rights of Passage kids, literally years.

And for each of these kids, all 44,000 of them around the country that we've seen this year, the love and faith and promise of our covenant finds a permanent resting place in their hearts. Truly, the love and hope you give these kids is as everlasting as it is infinite. I daresay there is no gift you could ever give or receive that means as much to so many in need.

So, as we end this year of saving kids, let me again say thank you. Thank you for helping us be there for Teresa in her greatest hour of need, and for 43,999 others in all of our shelters in the moments they needed someone to cling to.

And please also know that I am forever thankful for your part in our covenant. I couldn't make that promise to a little 12-year-old girl lying in a hospital bed, if it weren't for you. You are every bit as important to this covenant as I am. I am eternally grateful for what you give to these kids. Always.

And I never, ever stop thanking God you found us.

Chapter 2

"You can't split us up,"
the oldest said. "You can't."

"Please don't let anyone split us up, Sister. Please! My brothers and my one sister need me."

The teenage girl shivering on our doorstep grabbed her three little brothers and her sister and hugged them as hard as she could. It was pitch dark and frigid, one of the coldest nights I can ever remember at Covenant House.

The littler kids were so scared they would barely look at me. I wanted to throw my arms around all of them, but there were too many arms and legs and shivering bodies.

"Please come in," I said. "Let us help you," I said.

"OK," the oldest said, bracing herself against the wind. "But you can't split us up," she said. "We're a family."

The kids trudged inside, and slowly began to take their coats off. It was hard for them not to repeatedly bump into each other, they stood so close together. In the faint light of our room, I saw three young boys and a young girl huddled around a "big" sister who couldn't have been more than 19. The two littlest kids, barely 11 or 12, were covered with bruises.

"Let's get you cleaned up and warm," I said. "And is anyone hungry?" I said, knowing the answer. The littlest kid's eyes shot up at me, giving his hunger away.

"You can't split us up," the oldest said. "You can't." As she spoke, the kids began gripping onto each other even more.

"Why don't you all come to my office," I said. "We'll talk there." The 10 scared eyes, some of them dripping wet now, looked at me and said OK.

As soon as we got to my office, before I could even sit down, the oldest began to speak. "These are all my brothers and my sister," she said. "We've been out on the street by ourselves. We were told maybe you could help us," she said.

"We will," I said. "Can you tell me what happened?"

"My father ... our father ... he ... he threw us out of the house," she said. "He said he didn't want us anymore." The 11-year-old began crying a little more.

"What about your mother?" I said.

"She's dead," the oldest said. "She died a couple years ago. Ever since then ... ever since then my father hasn't wanted us around. Then two nights ago, he just threw us out. He said he was sick of us. He said, 'You're all old enough now — go out on your own.'"

"I'm so sorry," I said, feeling a little embarrassed that I didn't have something far more profound or comforting to offer them at that moment. I know, her eyes said.

During the next two hours, Nicole told me the rest of the story. How the kids had spent a frigid cold night huddled over a steam vent. How they had met a policeman who directed them to Covenant House. But most of all, she talked about her fear. Even though they were no longer hungry and cold, Nicole was consumed by a larger worry. Over and over she said....

>   *"Don't split us up. We're a family.*
>   *We're all we've got."*

"I'll do everything I can," I said. "Don't worry."

At last I convinced the children that they'd each see each other in the morning, and we led them off to bed. And then I went to sleep, wondering how we would keep these kids together.

I do know one thing — these kids *need* to be with each other. Instinctively. Emotionally. Desperately. They need to feel the touch of their siblings' hands, and hear the chatter of their siblings' voices, as much as they need oxygen to breathe.

In the time they have been here, they've become a living and breathing monument to family, a family mysteriously and beautifully tied together at the soul. If you call for one of them, they all come. If you ask one a question, they all nod in unison. At meals, they won't eat until they are all seated together. At night, they won't go to bed until they've all hugged each other good night.

They are lost, lonely, terrified and afraid, with a

thousand good reasons to simply fall apart and make life miserable for our shelter and our society. But they won't. They *can't*. Somewhere behind the wet eyes and uncertain steps, they've been instilled with an infinite belief in the power of "family."

Each child may have been stripped of the confidence to believe in themselves (God help me, I have trouble ever, ever forgiving their father for doing that to them!). But each child has never lost the faith to believe in each other.

Our little ragtag group of five homeless kids, aged 11 to 19, is one of the most beautiful demonstrations of family love I have ever seen. They're an inspiration to me. And a lesson to all of us.

I want you to know we are going to do all we can to keep these kids together as a family. We will, we will, we will. It's the covenant I've made with all these kids.

Things are falling into place as well as we could have hoped. (I'm sure God's hands are busier than ever orchestrating the whole thing!) We've already found a great home where all the three youngest kids can stay together. And we're making sure Nicole and her 18-year-old brother Fred get good jobs, right near where their siblings live, so they can always be close together. Nothing, but nothing, is going to ever break apart this incredibly beautiful family! They worked too hard to stay together.

Dear Heavenly Father,
Please give me the strength to go on through my
stay at Covenant House. Give me the wisdom and
the knowledge to do what is right and not wrong.
And please give me the strength to make the right
decisions about the things that occur. I know I
haven't been making the right decisions, but I'd
like to better that. Life has not been easy for me
through these times, but I know that you will give
me the strength to go on for I do believe in you
and all you say and do. Amen.

A prayer written
by a kid in our
Covenant House Chapel

Chapter 3

"It must be nice to be loved," she said.
"Do you believe in love?" she said.

Kids at Covenant House are a lot like snowflakes. Most of the time they manage to land softly on our doorstep, quietly, unannounced, without raising much of a stir.

But every once in a while they just seem to crash down on us in a never-ending avalanche, testing our already overstretched staff to the limits to keep up with the huge new pile of problems they've left on our doorstep.

January was one of those avalanche months here at Covenant House, both in snow and kids. The combination of snow and knee-deep drifts these last few weeks have forced hundreds of new kids to land on our doorstep, each kid knee deep in their own misery.

Thanks to you, we've managed to overcome this heaven-sent challenge pretty well. Just the other night, I was downstairs congratulating the staff on the great job they've done plowing ahead through pretty tough terrain.

Then, God led Ashley to our door.

And I don't feel as good anymore. I get a lump in my throat just thinking about her.

She came to our shelter about 8:30 or 9:00 on Tuesday. We're not really sure of the exact time because Ashley didn't knock at first. She just stood quietly outside and leaned against the building, in a corner where no one could see her.

Finally, when her feet were so frozen she couldn't feel them anymore, she leaned up against the front door.

"Hello," we said, when we saw her standing there. "Please, come in," we said. She didn't say anything. She didn't have to. The tears running down her face told us she was happy someone cared enough to welcome her inside.

During that first day, Ashley stayed to herself as much as she could, parceling out one word answers — "yes," "no," "uhuh" — to our counselors trying to help her. It wasn't that she was trying to be mean or impolite. She was clearly just too tired, too hurt, too crushed, too terrified and too overwhelmed to talk much. She didn't need words to communicate her pain. It cascaded over her like a flash blizzard.

Finally, this morning at the end of breakfast, I sidled up to her table and asked if she would like to talk. To my surprise, she nodded her head and motioned me to sit down.

"We'd really like to help you," I said. "Is there anything you'd like to talk to me about?"

For the longest time, she stared at me, wondering what to do. Should I trust you, her eyes kept asking. Will you understand me, her eyes said. Will anyone understand me? Then her mouth opened.

"I was just wondering," she said, in the tired voice of somone who didn't know what to believe in any more. "It must be nice to be loved," she said. "Do you believe in love?" she said.

She dropped her eyes the second I looked at her, and began rubbing a little green plastic box she carried in her knapsack. It was a hard question. It was a great question. I ached to know why she asked it.

"I do very much," I said. "I think it's the most beautiful and powerful emotion of all," I said. "I'm sure we'll all love you very much as we get to know you. Why do you ask?"

"Well, I've never been loved before," she said.

"Why do you say that," I said.

"No one's ever loved me," she said. "My parents ... my parents abandoned me. When I was 14. They definitely never loved me," she said.

"I'm so sorry," I said. "What happened?"

"It's not all that important," she said. "They just wanted to live life without me around, so they left," she said.

"What did you do then?"

"I ... I just tried to live. I slept in the houses of people I met or on the street. I tried to meet people who cared about me," she said. "I ... I even got a boyfriend. And ... and a baby," she said. The pain in her eyes began to gush out in tears and quietly dripped down her cheeks. She was just 18, 19 years old tops, and she looked like she was 200 years old.

"Where's your baby," I said.

"She's dead," she said.

"My boyfriend ... my boyfriend used to beat me. And then one day he ... he shook my little baby girl and killed her," she said. "He's in jail now."

"I'm so very sorry he did that," I said, as I reached out and hugged her. For the longest time she sat there in my arms and sniffled. I tried as hard as I could to comfort her, but I couldn't.

"I loved her," she said. "She was the only thing I ever had that I loved. I'm really having trouble living without her."

"You'll always have her here," I said, pointing to her head and then her heart. I know my words seemed so hollow at that moment, but I didn't know what else to say.

"I know," she said. "And I'll always have her here with me," she said, holding the green plastic box in her hands.

"Her ashes are inside this box," she said.

I thought at that moment I was going to cry, too. I didn't know what to say. There was really nothing more I could say. I just hugged her as hard as I could while she cried. We stayed there consoling each other for a long time, until a team of counselors came and gently took her to a room to rest.

I frankly don't know what to do with Ashley. She worries me greatly. There are some things it's hard to imagine a child recovering from — ever. Her parents abandoned her and her boyfriend murdered her baby.

How can any child ever recover from pain like that?
It's as if her heart has been burned from both ends.

Chapter 4

*"I slept in a subway the last 10 days
just to keep warm. I didn't know
how else to survive."*

I just saw God a few hours ago.

He came unannounced to our shelter, right before dinner, a not-too-tall, not-too-clean kid dressed in dirty sneakers and a rumpled dungaree jacket.

He was too tired and too beaten to say much on our doorstep.

"Hi," he said. "I don't have any place to stay, and I heard you can help me," he said. "I'm really feeling kinda sick. Can I get something to eat?"

And when I smiled and said, "Yes ... welcome ... please stay," he was almost too tired to mumble a thank you. He just rubbed his eyes, and smiled the best he could. You could see God etched on his face from a mile away.

I guess some people might think I'm a little crazy that I can see God in the face of a not-too-tall, not-too-clean street kid.

But I know you would have seen Him there too.

I mean, I think the most profound and beautiful and painful thing about being at Covenant House is the absolute bedrock realization that the kids on our doorstep have more in common with Jesus and know more about what He felt, and why He hurt, and how He suffered more than anyone else in this world. Certainly more than I ever, ever could....

Jesus wasn't exactly the most popular and revered figure of His time, at least among the power brokers and what passed for the movers and shakers.

Jesus was, like our kids, a wanderer and nomad, with no place to lay his head. Like most of our kids, He was born into poverty and welcomed by outcasts. He was no stranger to the intense hunger our kids feel, their searing fatigue, their rejection and self-wondering and pain.

When our not-too-tall, not-too-clean kid wakes up tomorrow, I'm sure he'll tell me things Jesus felt too. The kid in the dungaree jacket will tell me, with tears in his eyes, about being rejected and feeling forsaken. He'll tell me about wondering, "Why has this happened to me? Please, what did I do to deserve this?"

The kid in the dungaree jacket will tell me about a gnawing pain in his stomach which helped him to forget, at least for a few minutes, the gnawing doubt and fear he feels in his heart. He'll tell me he never knew where he would sleep from night to night. Who he could take comfort in. He'll look me in the eye and say something like, "I slept in a subway the last 10 days, just to keep warm. I didn't know how else to survive."

I think if they had subways 2,000 years ago, Jesus would have taken refuge there too. I know — I absolutely know — that our kids are among the people He loves the most, because He shares with them something that many of us will never, or can never, share with Him ourselves.

And I'm sure His love for them is extra, extra strong right now, during Lent.

I'm not the world's biggest fan of Lent. In fact, I really don't like it (it's not something we're supposed to like, I guess).

I mean, Lent is all about tough questions. It's all about things we must ask ourselves, and reckoning, and looking in the mirror and seeing if we like what's staring back at us.

It's a time to reflect on how we use the goods of the world and how we deal with our relationships. It's a time to think back if we're really trying to live a life of love, a time to look under the hood of our souls to make sure everything's running all right and see where the defects are.

Lent's also about resolutions to turn our lives around, and then begin the painful process of dealing with those resolutions....

Easy? It's not, and it's not supposed to be. It's not easy spending forty days staring into the mirrors of our souls, scrutinizing, writing checklists, grading performance. It's never easy asking ourselves if we're really being as good as we want to be, as virtuous, as steadfast, as understanding. But it's a good time for us, I think. Lent is the one time when we are most in touch with God.

Our kids? Kids like the not-too-tall, not-too-clean kid on my doorstep? I think they know all about Lent, and what God intended for Lent, better than most of us ever will. Our kids live in a perpetual Lent ... a non-stop life of painful reckoning, questioning, excruciating self-examination, of losses.

I mean, you and I may "give up things" for these next forty days by choice. Our kids have spent a lifetime "giving up things" ... things that no kid should ever have to give up.

They "give up" home because they've been battered and abused so much they simply can't live there anymore. In running to the street, they "give up" all hope of being loved. They "give up" all hope of being cared for. Of feeling secure. Of being loved.

Lent is truly in their hearts every minute of their lives.

It's not hard to see God in their wet eyes and tired faces. I know, I just know, you'd see Him there too.

"On the street I saw a girl cold and shivering in a thin dress, with little hope of a decent meal. I became angry and said to God: 'Why did you permit this? Why don't you do something about it?' For a while God said nothing. That night He replied quite suddenly: 'I certainly did something about it. I made you.'"

Chapter 5

"That's my last hope," his eyes said.
"I don't know anyone else, Sister."

"Here, Sister, try this phone number," the kid said, pulling a scrap of paper out of the bottom of his pocket.

"It's my Aunt Sharon. I lived with her for awhile. I really like her," he said. "I think she likes me. Maybe you could call her?"

I looked at the incredibly sad-looking and desperate 15-year-old boy rocking back and forth in front of me, and felt the tears welling up in my eyes.

I had already called Danny's mother to tell her that our street van had rescued Danny off the street and he needed a place to call home. "I can't handle having a kid again," she had told me.

I had already tried calling Danny's Aunt Karen, who told me she had three kids of her own and Danny was too much to handle.

I had already tried Danny's grandmother. Danny once lived with her for a year, but she said she was too old to raise a teenager.

So now we were down to Aunt Sharon.

"I think she kind of likes me," Danny said, rubbing his eyes and trying to hide his embarrassment. "Maybe you could call her, OK?" he said.

Danny got up from his chair and turned real fast and raced out of the room. We both knew at that moment why he was leaving my office. He was too afraid he might start crying in front of me. Too afraid to hear me desperately trying to convince someone to take him.

Too afraid to be embarrassed again in front of me because no one wants him. Too afraid to be rejected. Too afraid to be reminded, for the umpteenth time in his life, that absolutely no one wanted him or loved him or cared about him.

I swallowed hard and made the call. It was pretty much like all the others. "Yes, I know he's alone," a voice on the other end from another state said. "I know he's a good kid. But, Sister, I got three of my own," she said. "I can't help him anymore," she said. "Why don't you try these other people," she said, naming all the people I'd already talked to. "I've got to go now," she said.

As I hung up the phone, Danny appeared at the doorway, huge pools of water glazed over his eyes. He didn't say anything. He didn't have to. His eyes at that moment were like an open book.

"Now what," his eyes said. "That's my last hope," they said. "I don't know anyone else, Sister," his eyes were screaming. "I've been passed around between five houses ever since my parents split up when I was eight," they said. "What's wrong with me? Am I that bad?

"Will anyone want me," his eyes said.

I put my arm around him, and told him how much we all loved him and how much we hoped he would stay with us. He was too tired, too beaten, too embarrassed, too ashamed, too sick, too numb and too devastated to say anything, but I know it meant a lot to him.

He is 15 and he's completely alone, and he's been passed around from house to house like a used book ever since his parents split.

And worst of all, he knows deep in his heart that no one wants him. As hard as we try to help him, as much as we love him, that feeling will gnaw at him and eat away at him. We're all he's got now. The world — his own little piece of the world — has looked him over and decided to take a pass on him.

I'm not sure what I'm going to tell him tonight when I see him again. I mean, there aren't a lot of words that will mean that much to him right now.

I think maybe the best thing we can ever do is just be there, to hear his agony, to comfort his tears, to forgive his anger, to understand his rage. And hopefully one day soon, when the scars have begun to heal, he will let us begin to help him rebuild his life, find a new home and find the love and happiness every kid deserves.

Chapter 6

"It's too dangerous for me at home," she said. "I'm afraid they might kill me."

The two desperate eyes locked in on me from across the room, and then began barreling toward me like a runaway train.

When the girl with those eyes got within five feet of me, she leapt airborne and literally affixed herself to me, squeezing me as tightly as she could.

"Please," she screamed out. "Don't let them do it," she screamed. "Please don't ... I'm afraid they'll kill me ... you don't understand ... don't let me go ... don't let me go ... don't let me go."

All the time she screamed, her body kept shaking and her arms kept squeezing, tighter and tighter until I could barely breathe. I was so overwhelmed, I had to drop the phone I held in my hand. If I live to be a hundred, I don't think I'll ever see a more terrified child.

Her name is Joy. Just three hours ago, Joy landed on our doorstep, a shy, timid, frail, all-alone kid carrying the trademark belongings of someone who had just run away from home (in other words, she had nothing but the clothes on her back).

"Could I come in," she had whispered on our

doorstep, ever so politely.

When we had said yes, her gratitude poured out like a dam bursting. "Thanks," she said. "You're really nice," she said. "Thanks for helping me," she said.

During her first few hours here, she did anything and everything we asked of her.

"My name is Joy," she quickly said, the moment we asked.

"Yes, I used to have a place to live, but I don't anymore," she told us the second we asked.

"This was my phone number," she said, rattling off a number from a town only 20 minutes from our shelter. "But that doesn't matter anymore," she said.

She was incredibly sweet, charming and proper. I'd never met a kid who was so polite and so thankful to be sitting in a shelter for homeless kids.

But then it happened.

"I'd like to call your parents," I said, reaching for the phone. "They must be very worried about you," I had said.

It was at that moment that Joy's eyes had flashed terror, and Joy raced across the room screaming.

Once I was able to calm her down a bit, I began to understand why she was so scared.

"Please understand, Sister," she said. "It's too dangerous for me at home. I'm afraid. They might kill me."

At that moment, she turned away from me, and lifted up her shirt a few inches. "These welts are from my parents," she said referring to the huge black and blue marks, and scars which covered most of her back. "They get very mad at me when I'm bad. So they take out a belt and hit me with it until I bleed." Her back was so bruised and bloodied, I had to catch my breath.

"What do you mean, bad?" I said.

"Oh, you know, like if I don't make my bed the right way," she said. "Or, like yesterday I left some dishes in the sink without putting them into the dishwasher." Tears began to well up in her eyes as she spoke. She looked about eight years old at that moment, standing there very embarrassed and unsure about what she was saying.

I reached out and hugged her as delicately as I could.

"I'm so sorry this happened to you," I said. "You don't deserve this. No kid does. I'm going to take care of this," I said.

She looked up at me with one of those "really?" expressions, and I saw hope flash in her eyes for the first time. "Thank you," she said. "Thank you." And then, for the next 10 minutes, she wept in my arms.

I don't know quite what else to tell you in this letter. I mean, I'm feeling a heartache and an anger and a frustration I don't often feel. I do want you to know that the moment I left Joy, I called the number she had given me. My conversation didn't improve my mood any....

"You've got my daughter," the woman on the other line said. "I want her back. Now."

"She's been abused," I told her. "What happened?"

I asked her.

"She's been bad," the voice on the other end said. "She deserved a little extra discipline," the voice said. "Abuse is a form of discipline," she said. I won't tell you how, but please know I spelled out my feelings on the responsibilities of parenthood very clearly.

As for Joy? I'm not letting her go back there. Never, never, never. I've already called the authorities and Child Protective Services, and first thing tomorrow, I'm going to do what I can to get her into a much more loving and nurturing environment.

And until then, we will love her and console her, and help her as much as we can. She will always, always know that she is loved, as long as she's here.

And when she's feeling better in a day or two, I'm going to tell her about wonderful people like you. As you can imagine, her faith in adults probably isn't what it could be right now. I'm going to make sure that she realizes there are lots of very wonderful and caring people like you who love her every bit as much as I do.

I know when I tell her it will bring a huge smile to her face. I smile every time I get to say it....

Help Me

Help me, Dear Lord,
     as I travel towards You.
There are many detours
     which will try to distract
     me away from You.
Help me as I travel my path
     to cherish the parents You gave me.
Help me to do my best in all my endeavors
     whether I may win or lose.
Help me never to lose hope
     though there may be difficult times.
Help me to choose good friends.
Help me to choose the right mate,
     so that I may have a happy family someday.
Help me, though I may fall,
     to continue on my journey towards You.
Help me, Dear Lord.
I want so much to be with You. Amen.

                    Written by a
                    Covenant House kid

Chapter 7

**"I guess it was my own
stupid fault to be sleeping
in that car," he said.**

"It looks pretty gross, doesn't it, Sister," the boy said pointing to his feet. "They had to take all five of my toes off this foot, but I only lost two on this one...."

He looked at me while he sat, trying to look brave, but not doing it very well. Eddie was only 17, but he looked about a hundred at that moment, a beaten, frustrated, desperate kid wondering why his life was falling apart before it ever had a chance to begin.

"It's kind of funny," he said rubbing his bare feet in the sunshine. "It used to be I couldn't even look at my feet," he said. "But I guess I gotta do it," he said. "I mean, I gotta accept the fact I'm kind of a cripple now," he said.

"Right?"

His voice trailed off and he sneaked a peak over at me. I started to tell him how he was still a strong, healthy boy, and he had a whole life in front of him, but he cut me off before I could get much out.

"I mean, I guess that's the way it goes sometimes," he said. "I mean, some kids live in houses and some don't. I guess it was my own stupid fault to be sleeping in that car," he said.

"It wasn't your fault, Eddie," I said. "What happened to you was very unfair," I said. "You did all you could do," I said.

"Well ... it wasn't enough, was it?" he said. "And now I'm left with this," he said, pointing to his feet and his crutches.

He came into our lives back in early April, another very tragic example of what happens to street kids who have no place to sleep in the winter.

Abandoned by his father at birth and by his mother at the age of 16, Eddie was left totally and completely alone this past winter with no place to escape.

During the bone-chilling nights in January and February, Eddie somehow managed to survive, spending the coldest nights riding New York's subway system or curled up next to a grate on a city street.

In March, when all of us began to hope the interminable winter of '96 was over, Eddie found refuge in an abandoned car. The cold he endured in that ice covered car was what you might experience climbing Mount Everest. Except mountain climbers are equipped with warm clothes, shoes and special equipment for their journey.

All Eddie had was a tattered coat and a pair of sneakers. And it wasn't enough.

One March night, when his feet had frozen so badly he couldn't feel them anymore, Eddie limped five blocks to a hospital, asking if he could just come inside to "warm up."

Within a few hours, he was on an operating table, losing most of his toes.

Within a few weeks, he came to us for the simple and painful reason that Eddie had absolutely no where else he could go.

Now, when the summer sun shines, Eddie goes outside and sits, warming his feet, wondering what to do next.

And every time I see him out there, my heart aches. Today, it just seemed to be aching a little more than usual....

"Eddie," I said while we sat together this morning on that stoop. "I'm so sorry for what has happened," I said. "But we'd like to help you," I said. "There's a wonderful doctor who's been a great friend to Covenant House. I've told him about you. I told him what a great kid you are. He said he'd love to work with you, get you special shoes and help you walk again."

It wasn't the first time I had brought this up with Eddie, but it seemed like the right moment to try again. I kept praying to God as the words spilled out — "Please God, let Eddie say 'yes' this time. Let his new life begin to begin."

Eddie was silent for the longest time as I spoke. We're used to that. He's not a kid who talks a lot. When he finally turned his face to me, there were tears in his eyes. I was shocked. For all Eddie has been through, I've never seen him break down and cry.

"I'd like to see him," he said. "I guess I'm ready

now," he said.

"Thank you," he said. "For everything."

That was all he said. We sat there together for a few minutes more, God's glorious sun beating down on us, both lost in our own thoughts, both consumed with our own fervent hopes for Eddie.

Chapter 8

"I don't think I'm worth the trouble," he said.

As soon as we opened the door, he leaned inside and dropped straight to our shelter floor.

He was a teenage boy, dressed in old and wet and tired clothes. Judging from his wind-burned, red face, he had probably been walking around in the winter's cold since early that morning. We didn't know what color his eyes were because they were barely open a crack. Fatigue hung from him like 1,000-pound weights.

"Thank you," he mumbled from the floor, so softly we could barely hear him. "Thank you. It's really ... it's really cold out there," he whispered.

"I need help," he whispered.

Our staff huddled around him, and helped him to a soft couch. He was barely 5'5" tall, but his cold and dripping clothes made him so heavy, it took four of us to lift him.

"Let us help you," I said as we lifted him onto the couch. "I'm so glad you found us," I whispered. "We're going to take good care of you," I said.

He pried his eyes open a crack and tried to send me a smile, but he was too tired to pull it off. "Thanks" was all he could say.

"Is it OK if I just lay here and sleep," he slurred.

"Sure, as soon as we get you into some dry, warm clothes."

He looked and sounded and acted like someone who was drunk, but he wasn't. He was just a tired and scared and absolutely exhausted kid, who I figured probably hadn't had a good night's sleep in four days. (As it turns out, my guess was off a little. After he finally woke up a day and a half later, I learned he hadn't slept in almost six!)

When he finally did wake up, we made sure he had a hot shower, some clean, comfortable clothes and some huge platefuls of food (he ate four).

While he was devouring his last helping of chicken and mashed potatoes, I sat down to see if he wanted to talk.

To my shock, he was one of those kids who was literally dying to pour out his heart to someone....

"My name is Dan," he said.

"I'm 18," he said, knowing as he said it that he was beaten and worn and tired enough to look like an old man.

"I've been on the street since I was 14," he said. "I had no other choice," he said. "Once I told my parents I was gay, they told me I wasn't welcome in their house anymore," he said. His eyes began to mist when he talked about his parents.

"That must have been so hard," I said. "I'm so sorry. How have you been able to survive?" I said.

"I'm no good, Sister," he said. "I mean, I am good, but I'm not. I mean ... I did ... I did what I had to do to live," he said.

"I think you know what I mean," he said.

I nodded my head, and felt my own tears welling inside. "I'm not as bad as they said I was," he emphasized while biting his lip. "I know you're not," I said.

"I'm sorry about the way I came here," he said, wanting to change the subject. "I must have looked like a real nerd, falling inside like that. I ... you gotta understand that I was just so tired, and I didn't have any place to go," he said.

"I'm really glad you came," I said. "Don't you worry about anything," I said. "I'm really hoping you'll stay with us. We'll help you get your life back together."

He looked at me for the longest time, trying to decide if I meant it, if in his world filled with people who don't care and can't be trusted that I was someone who was actually a little different than all the others he had known. His mind was racing so fast and so hard, I could almost see the wheels turning inside his watery eyes.

"I don't think so," he finally said with a quiet sigh. "I don't think I'm worth the trouble," he said. "Thanks anyway," he said.

Before I could blurt out how wrong he was, he bolted out of his chair and began to race out of the cafeteria. "Think about it," I yelled out. "We want to help you." He turned slightly, waved his right hand as

if to say, "I'll think about it," and then bolted into the
hallway....

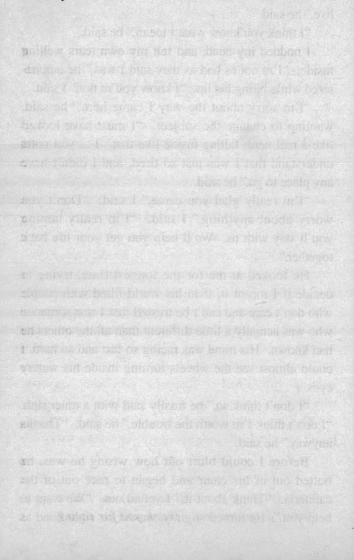

Chapter 9

*"They'll never forgive me
for what I've done," she said.
"That's why I had to run away."*

"I had to give you this myself," she said breathlessly. "I know it's early, but would you open it now?

"I've been dying to give you this for a long, long time."

It was a cold, rainy night, the weekend before Christmas. Covenant House was in its usual pre-Christmas state of pandemonium. I was up to my eyeballs in problems. I wanted to get back to my office.

Little did I know I was about to get one of the best Christmas gifts of my life.

"Here, please take this," the nicely dressed young woman urged me, handing me the box. The adorable little boy whose hand she held jumped up and down with delight. I had no idea who they were, no idea why they had come, no idea what was about to happen.

The box seemed to hold only tissue paper. Then I found a card. And inside the card, a check for $100.

*"Merry Christmas," the card began. "I
don't know if you remember me, but I have
never forgotten you. Thank you for saving*

me and my boy Brendan. Merry Christmas!
Love, your 'Cat' from long, long ago."

"Cat?" I exclaimed in disbelief. "Cat? It's really you?"

"Yes, it's me!" she laughed, tears rolling down her cheeks. As we exchanged hugs, I tried to match her glowing, healthy face with that of a sad and pale street child from five years ago.

"And this is Brendan," she said, stroking the hair of the little boy. "Brendan, this is Sister Mary Rose. She helped me when I had a lot of problems before you were born.

"Now it's my turn to help her."

I'll never forget the first time I met Catherine. Five winters ago we found her pregnant, starving and shivering — and trying to live inside a cardboard box at the back of a Manhattan alley.

She had been living in that box for five months!

When I learned her nickname was "Cat," I thought, "Stray Cat." I always remember her that way.

"I need someplace warm to sleep," she said that first time I met her. "Just for one night, then I'll be all right," she said. Her denim jacket, wet with the winter's snow, was torn in three places. It looked like she hadn't taken a bath in weeks.

After we got her medical treatment and prenatal care, I kept urging her to call her parents. "I can't do that," she kept saying. "I let them down," she said. "They'll never forgive me for what I've done," she said.

"That's why I had to run away."

But she was wrong. I can still see her on the phone that winter's evening when she finally found the courage to call her mom and dad. Five seconds into the conversation, I could hear shrieks of joy screaming out of the phone. Ten seconds into the conversation, I knew that this beautiful lost child was about to find her way back.

The next day, we put Catherine on a plane to California, and sent her home. "I'll repay you someday for everything," she kept saying on the way to the airport. "I can't thank you enough," she said.

I didn't hear much from Catherine after that, except that she had given birth to a healthy baby, and had settled back at home.

Until the weekend before Christmas. I still can't get over it. I smile every time I think about it.

I hope you're smiling as you read this, too. I mean, I know it sometimes seems like we're fighting the tide or the wind. We keep doing the best we can, when we can, but sometimes, some days it just doesn't seem like enough.

But then you meet a girl like Catherine, holding a beautiful child's hand in one arm and a box filled with love in the other, and you know that your love is saving lives. For every Catherine who stood on my doorstep Christmas Eve weekend, there were thousands and thousands and thousands like her who sat quietly at home, surrounded by loved ones, thanking God for you and the help you gave them when they most needed it many years ago.

True, we haven't saved all 400,000 plus kids who've turned to us this last quarter century. You and I both know that. But somewhere out there, thousands of young adults are living safe, productive, hope-filled lives because of what we've done together. Please, don't ever forget that. I know that God never will....

"I'll repay you for everything someday," she told me one day five years ago. *"I can't thank you enough,"* she had said.

I feel so very blessed that God gave me this chance to know Catherine. And you. Thank you again so very much. I never, ever stop thanking God you found us.

Chapter 10

"I guess they were too stubborn to let me die," he said.

"I used to do drugs," the young man in the neatly pressed business suit told me.

"I used to eat out of dumpsters and sleep on the street too," he said.

"I just had to come back to say 'thank you'" he said, the hint of a very large tear beginning to well in his eye.

"I know ... I know...," he said quickly, before I could even respond. "I know you don't remember me ... I was just one of a million kids ... it was five years ago ... I wasn't anything special," he said.

"I can still remember the first second I met you guys," he said, taking another step forward into our shelter. "Could I sit down here while I talk ... is that OK?" he said.

I smiled and nodded and sat down beside him. By this time I had figured out that this great kid in the business suit was more than anything in the world dying to blurt out his story, as quickly and as passionately as he could.

I decided the tears beginning to form in my eyes were all he needed to hear from me.

"It was your rescue van that started it all," he said.

"I was walking in Times Square that night all alone, thinking maybe I should just kill myself," he said. "I mean it was *that* bad, I was *that* low," he said. He bit off the two "thats" for extra emphasis. I nodded to let him know I understood exactly how desperate he was.

"The lady in your van ... gee, I wish I could remember her name now ... she asked me if I wanted some hot chocolate and a sandwich," he said. "I was so hungry my whole body hurt, but I said 'no.' I was afraid to trust her, I was afraid to trust anyone.

"Five minutes later the van pulled around again, and the lady inside rolled down the window, and stuck out a sandwich. 'Please, take this. You look really hungry,' she said. I couldn't believe that someone would care enough to keep asking," he said. "So I took it.

"We talked for a long time that first night," he said. "The snow and wind were brutal, but I was afraid to get inside the van. I said thanks and left. I figured I'd never see you guys again."

A smile came to his lips while he thought about that first night. It was the same kind of smile you get when you think about the first moment you laid eyes on your newborn child, or that smile you get the moment before you see a young kid you love walk down the aisle to get married. His smile was that kind of smile — a smile celebrating the day he got his life back.

"Your staff was pretty persistent," he said, laughing. "They came right back to the same spot the next night. I guess they were too stubborn to let me die.

"I finally said I'd go back to Covenant House," he

said. "I figured I'd get a good night's sleep and some food, and then leave. But once I got here ... once they started talking to me, I couldn't leave," he said. The tears began to spill out of his eyes. He didn't seem to mind crying in front of me. I think somehow, deep down, he was proud of his tears.

"The first couple of weeks were like being in another world," he said. "I mean, I had lived on the street for two years, Sister — I had to — my father beat me at home — I didn't have any choice but to run away," he said. "It was so strange being here. I wasn't used to feeling human," he said.

He didn't have to explain to me what he meant. I'd heard the story so many times before — the story of how degrading and awful and dispiriting and terrifying living on the street eventually becomes for a kid — so I knew exactly where he was coming from. From a very sad and dark place....

"One day, though, it all just clicked inside me," he said. "All of a sudden I realized that you guys really did care about me. That I was worth something.

"I leaned on you pretty hard for help," he said with a smile. "I took all the classes you would give me. I spent hours and hours working on the computer you had ... I got a job thanks to you," he said. "It was just an entry level job, but it was a start. And now...." he said, smiling from ear to ear, "Now I sell computers for a living," he said. "And I'm doing great.

"I just wanted you to know that," he said.

"I mean, I actually went to your candlelight vigil in

December to tell you that," he said. "But I got so
choked up that night, and it was so crowded, I just never
got to see you," he said. "I can still hear them singing
'Amazing Grace' that night. All the time it was being
sung, I kept thinking what an Amazing Grace my life
has become.

"I don't want to take up any more of your time," he
said. "Look at all these other kids you got here today,"
he said. "Here, please let me give you this to help some
of these other kids," he said, handing me two crisp $20
bills.

He stood up, leaned over and kissed me on the top
of the head. "Thank you for everything. By the way,
my name is Michael ... I'll see you again someday," he
said.

"Thanks so much, Michael," I said. "Come back,
and we'll talk some more," I said, smiling, knowing that
I hadn't said anything the whole 10 minutes he was
here.

"I'd like that," he said, smiling back. And with that,
the sharp-looking, young kid in the neatly pressed suit
walked out of the door.

"Wow," I said, still drinking it all in.

"Thank you, God," I said.

Our Love

Sometimes I wonder how people
    judge our love,
They never seem to notice that it
    comes from Heaven above.
But if our love is strong and true
    and solid to the soul,
Then listening to them is not
    what we'll do.
Our love will be bold.
The love we have will shine
    through storms,
No matter how rough the times.
Forever and ever, we'll be
    together like the sun.
Yes, it will shine.

        Written by a
        Covenant House kid

Chapter 11

*"I used to be from somewhere,
but I'm not from anywhere
anymore," she said.*

"I heard that you could help me," she said.

"Maybe you could just let me have a sandwich, and I'll get out of your hair," she said.

"I really don't want to get in your way."

I looked into her sad, no-one-loves-me eyes, and felt a stake piercing through my heart. She was a little kid, maybe 14 or 15 or 16 dressed in blue jeans and a sweatshirt that should have been thrown into a trash heap months ago. She was one of those street urchins we see so often, the kind of vagabond/bump-around/hard-knocks kid who mysteriously appears at our doorstep all of a sudden, covered with filth and oozing neglect.

I actually had a hard time guessing her age, there was so much dirt and pain smeared across her face.

But there was no mistaking her sweetness and her goodness. Even in the twilight of an early spring evening, we could see those qualities from a mile away. You would have loved her the second you laid eyes on her....

"Maybe I could even get a little something to drink too," she said. "If it wouldn't be a problem?"

"Please, come in," I said. "We've got plenty of food. Please, we're glad you are here," I said.

She tried to smile back, but I could tell she wasn't too used to smiling. She nodded a small nod, and quickly walked in.

"There's a cafeteria down the hall," I said. "Why don't we just take a minute to wash our hands and get cleaned up, and I'll take you there myself," I said. "My name is Sister Mary Rose — what's yours?" I said.

"Dana," she said.

"Where are you from," I said.

"Nowhere," she said.

"What do you mean," I said.

"Well ... I mean I used to be from somewhere, but I'm not from anywhere anymore," she said. "Is this the way to the cafeteria," she said.

I took her by the hand, and led her to a sink and a bar of soap, where she could clean off the layers of dirt camped out on her hands and arms. It wasn't a simple cleaning — it was a good forty-five seconds before I could see her red, chafed skin underneath. Once her hands were dried, I hurried her to the cafeteria, where hot soup and sandwiches were lined neatly on the countertops.

Dana grabbed three of each, rushed politely over to the first empty table, and dove in. It took her all of five minutes to clean off the entire tray.

"Thanks a lot," she said. "That was really good," she said. "Maybe I can come back again," she said, half-asking, half-telling, totally hoping I'd say 'yes.'

"You're welcome to stay now," I said. "We've got plenty of clean beds (plenty was a tiny exaggeration, because we're crammed with kids right now, but I was trying to convince her to stay as hard as I could), and you're welcome."

She fidgeted with the napkin, not quite knowing what to say. I could tell she was beginning to get interested....

"Tell me a little about yourself," I said. "How old are you?"

"Sixteen," she said.

"Is there someone we can call to let them know you're here," I said.

"There used to be," she said. "But not anymore."

"What do you mean," I said. "I'd like to help you," I said.

For the longest time, Dana looked at me, twisting her napkin, trying to decide a hundred things all at once. Should I talk? Or should I go? Can I trust this lady? What is this place? Why am I here? How did this happen? Is this someone I can believe in? Where am I going to sleep tonight if I don't sleep here? What should I do? A hundred questions ... all of them way too serious and heartbreaking and urgent for a 16-year-old kid to have to worry about.

Finally, the tears began to form in her eyes, and she decided to take a chance. Dana decided to trust in us.

"I used to live in a real house," she said. "I had a mother and a father and five brothers," she said. "That was a long time ago," she said.

"Then, last year, my dad decided to leave. He just walked out one day ... he didn't even tell me he was going anywhere ... he just left.

"My mother ... my mother couldn't take it anymore. She tried to get a job ... but it all got to be too much.

"About two months ago, she sat me down and told me I had to leave. 'You're 16, Dana,' she said. 'You're the oldest ... I can't afford all of you ... you're going to have to leave.'

"I looked at her like she was kidding. I mean, leave for what, Sister? Go where? I'm 16 ... it's not like I know a million places to go.

"But my mother kept telling me I had to get out," Dana said. "'You can make it, Dana,' my mother said. 'You're strong like me. Pack up your things. I'm sorry, you have to go.' "

As she poured out her story, the tears began rolling down Dana's cheeks in streams. They were the angry, pained, disbelieving tears of a 16-year-old girl who suddenly found herself all alone, on the street, by herself. I grabbed her hand and told her again how glad I was she had found us. She cried some more, and tried to keep on talking....

"At first ... at first I thought I could make it. I met a boy on the street the first day. I thought maybe I could live with him.

"But ... but that didn't work out ... it ... it didn't work out."

"Where have you been living," I said.

"Around," she said. "You know, places," she said, street kid shorthand for alleys, subways, park benches and any other place where a kid can find a spot to sleep.

"We'd love to have you stay with us," I said. "We've got plenty of room," I said.

"I think I'd like that," she said. And then she began to sob uncontrollably. It was a long time before she could stop.

I made sure our staff took extra special care of Dana tonight. We got her some brand-new pajamas, and I made sure she got a room right near one of her counselors, so she could see someone by her all night.

I'm not sure how, or if, she'll be able to sleep tonight.

I mean, I know she's exhausted. She probably hasn't had a restful moment since she was kicked out of her home. But the questions pouring through her head, bouncing back and forth ... I'm sure they're keeping her up tonight.

"How did I ever end up here?" her mind must be asking her. "What did I do wrong? Am I going to always be alone? Am I ever going to be OK? Can I trust these people here? Can I ever trust anyone? Why doesn't my mom love me? Why doesn't anyone love me? Will anyone ever love me?"

I do know one thing. We're going to do everything humanly possible to help her, and try to rebuild her life (and as we're doing all we humanly can, I'm going to be praying extra hard to God for His help too).

I mean, with all the awful, tough, gut-wrenching questions Dana has facing her tonight, the one question she will never have to ask is — "Can I find hope here?"

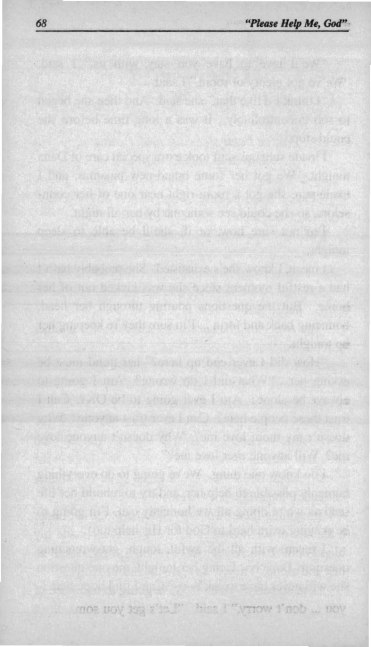

Chapter 12

"We've been sleeping under piles of leaves at night," he said.

"Please help us, Sister," the first crying kid said. "It's awful out there.

"Me and my brother have been living outside," he said, putting his arms around a sobbing little boy. "We've been sleeping under piles of leaves at night.

"We can't take it anymore," the bigger kid said. "We ... just ... can't ... take ... it."

The two kids glanced in my direction for another second, and then buried their heads in their hands. They were two of the wettest, most miserable looking kids I've ever seen.

Streams of water poured down their soaking hair, past their wet faces and careened into their damp, used-to-be-white sweatshirts. Every time they moved (and they kept turning their eyes away to sneak a peak at the usual bedlam of 20 or so kids lined up in our shelter entrance), their old shoes squeaked.

Imagining these two kids, curled up together under a blanket of wet leaves in the cold night air made my blood boil. I wanted to hug them both, they looked so lost and alone. They were really beautiful kids....

"I'm so sorry," I said. "We're going to take care of you ... don't worry," I said. "Let's get you some clean clothes and some food and medicine right away," I said.

"And we've got plenty of warm beds," I said, although maybe "plenty" was an exaggeration since we've been absolutely swamped with kids this month. "I bet you two would love to have a good night's sleep," I said.

"Yeah," the first kid stammered, through his tears. The younger brother looked at me to pass along his thanks, too. He was too choked up to speak.

In a jiffy, an army of staff and volunteers swarmed over the kids and whisked them off. I didn't see either of them until the next day. After showering, eating and wrapping themselves inside some warm clothes, the two fell into bed and just slept for the next 14 hours. We're guessing it was the first civilized sleep they had enjoyed in weeks.

About two hours ago, I finally got a chance to catch up with them again after lunch.

"I really want to thank you," the first one said. "We really needed this," he said.

"Yeah, it's been really great," the younger one said. "It's too bad we have to go, right, Billy?" he said, looking at his bigger brother.

Sitting there at the time, all relaxed and dry for the first time, the younger kid looked even younger now, a baby almost, maybe 14 years old tops.

"Going?" I said. "But where? Do you have someone I can call to pick you up?"

The two glanced at each other, and began relaying those unspoken, imperceptible, unmistakable body signals that develop as language between two brothers.

"Yeah, we have someone," they said, nodding their heads in unison. "It's our mother," the older one said. "She's waiting for us," he said, not too convincingly.

"Where is she," I said. "She must be worried. Let's call her," I said.

"She's around," the older one said. "Yeah, around," the younger one said. "We'll find her, no problem."

"Do you have an address," I said. "We can take you there to find her."

The two kids looked again at each other, but the self-assuredness, so evident a minute ago, was now gone. The older boy, Billy, who was 16, rubbed his hands over his forehead. The 14 year old, David, seeing that his chief protector was now upset, got all choked up again....

I put my hands over their hands and tried to console them. It was a good three minutes before Billy could muster up the strength to talk. What he told me didn't make me feel any better....

"Our mother ... she lost her job ... a while ago," he said. "And then ... then we got kicked out of our apartment last week.

"We didn't have a place to stay ... but we were able to stay in a motel for one night until the money ran out," he said. "Then Mom told us she could earn some money for us at the motel ... she asked us to leave for a couple of days." (The pain in his eyes made it clear how his mother was planning on earning the money the family needed.)

"What happened next," I said.

"We slept in the woods down the street for a while, then we went back to find her. She wasn't around ... we didn't know where she was ... we didn't know what to do. A guy we ran into said there was this place called Covenant House, so we hitchhiked here."

All the time the 16 year old spoke, the younger brother just sat there with his hands over his ears, grimacing. The whole mess was too much to hear, let alone bear.

"Our mom *is* there, Sister," Billy said. "We've *got* to get to her," he said. His words just made David choke up a little more.

A few minutes ago we called the motel looking for Billy and David's mother. The gruff, detached manager at the motel didn't offer much help or information. We're still not sure where she is or what's going to happen next.

I wish I had more, and better, news to share with you....

Chapter 13

*"I guess I thought
I wasn't worth it," she said.*

"I was floating face down in the water, Sister, pretending I was dead.

"I was so scared, Sister, I was so scared," she said, trembling. "I was bleeding real bad ... she had shot me twice.

"I wanted to scream out for help. But I knew if I moved at all, she would shoot me again. I could feel her watching me.

"So I just floated, pretending I was dead.

"I think deep down I was *hoping* I was dead.

"I figured maybe I deserved it, right?"

The 18-year-old girl looked up at me from her hospital bed, with tubes running out of her arms and a look of disbelief stamped across her face. I think she was having trouble believing what she was saying. I was having trouble believing her words too. *"I was floating face down in the water,"* this skinny kid was telling me. *"She had shot me twice. I was pretending I was dead. I hoped I was dead. Maybe I deserved it,"* she was saying.

"I'm so glad you made it," I said. "Please don't ever say you deserve to die. You're a good girl, Kim. I really believe in you," I said.

She looked up at me, a little surprised that someone

actually cared that much. "Well ... I guess I just thought I wasn't worth it," she said.

"I mean, Sister, I've done some pretty dumb things," she said. "Really dumb...."

I should tell you in advance that Kim is the last kid I'd ever expect to hear this story from. I mean, she's not a "rough-tough" street kid you might expect to get in trouble. She's a meek, skinny, shy girl from the farm-belt in Missouri who never forgets to say "yes, ma'am" and "please" and "thank you."

Unfortunately, Kim has never forgotten something else — an awful, pain-filled childhood. She never knew her father — he died when Kim was a baby. But she's known two stepfathers in her short life. The first one abused her sexually. As so often happens, she was afraid to tell anyone about it. It was her secret wound, festering in her soul.

By the time her mother remarried again Kim was so angry, so depressed, so scarred, so hurt, that she ached to escape her own private hell.

And so, like thousands of girls every year, Kim ran away with a man who "promised to love her and take care of her." Except the second they arrived in the city, this man took her money and dumped her. Leaving Kim all alone. Penniless. Absolutely terrified.

I'm sure you can guess for yourself what happened next.

Kim met another "great guy," this one named Bill, who promised to "take care of her." Of course, after a few days, Bill forced Kim to put on some cheap lipstick and cheaper clothes and to walk the streets as a prostitute.

It was then, finally, that Kim was able to escape her loneliness and terror on the street, when she found Covenant House.

Kim spent two weeks with us. We were so thrilled she found us. I mean, it was impossible not to fall in love with her. She was one of those great kids you just naturally love.

Unfortunately, one afternoon right after lunch, Kim's trusting nature got the best of her....

"I decided to go back to Bill's place to get my clothes. I mean, I just wanted to run in, grab what I owned and run out. But this older lady was there when I arrived.

"This lady said she was Bill's 'partner' ... that she and Bill had been looking for me ... that they were afraid I was going to go to the police and tell them about what Bill was doing.

"So this lady pointed a gun at me, and made me get in her car. Then she drove me outside of town, pulled me down to the riverbank, and shot me twice, until she thought I was dead."

I think it's a miracle that Kim somehow survived this nightmare. But somehow ... somehow she was able to pull herself out of the stream, crawl to a road and flag down help. By the time the truck driver had rushed Kim to the hospital, she was in such bad shape that the doctor had to remove her spleen.

Kim spent 10 long days in the hospital. As she lay

there in that bed, tubes crawling out her arms, her body weak, her heart torn apart, Kim and I had a lot of time to talk about her life, her hopes, her dreams.

And it was there that a kid who had almost died was reborn.

"You know what, Sister," she said one night I'll never forget.

"Don't laugh at what I'm going to say ... but I think I'm lucky. I mean, I could be dead ... I actually wanted to die ... but God has given me a second chance."

"If it's OK with you, can I get a chance to talk to the other kids when I get back? I mean, I think I can really help them," she said.

I had trouble answering her at first. I had this big lump in my throat. "I think that would be great, Kim," I said. "As soon as you get better."

Last night, at 9:15 PM, a skinny kid with a bullet still in her side, stood up before a roomful of kids and talked to them about almost dying, and feeling like dying, and wanting to die, and the beauty of discovering how really beautiful it is after all to live.

The kids listened about as intently as I've ever seen our kids listen. Dying is a subject these kids think about a lot. It's not a hypothetical thing, but something they can feel and taste — something they actually consider a lot because their lives can be so very hard.

I know it really helped them to hear Kim tell them how beautiful and precious life really is. In sharing her story, I think she was giving a piece of life to all of them. It was one of the most touching and beautiful things I've ever seen....

Thank you, thank you, thank you so much for being part of this wonderful, beautiful story of life and hope! In many ways Kim's story is a living and breathing testament to your love and what Covenant House is all about.

Ultimately we are driven by a belief — an unmistakable and irrefutable knowledge — that life is precious, that every child is a gift from God, that we must do all we can to protect and love and save these most innocent and lost of his children.

I really think that it was your love, and this profound commitment on your part, that gave Kim the strength to pull herself out of that river, to crawl to the road and to choose life over death.

And it will be that love and commitment, now forever instilled in Kim's heart, that is giving more kids the strength and courage to go on.

Thank you so very, very much for this gift of life you have helped give Kim. I know that she will never, ever forget what you have done for her.

Chapter 14

*"He told me to get out.
He said as far as he was
concerned, I was dead."*

"He just wouldn't forgive me, that's the part that
hurts the most. Why wouldn't he forgive me?

"I know I made a mistake, Sister. I know that. I
said I was sorry. I said it over and over again.

"But it didn't seem to make any difference.

"I was a good kid, Sister. Really I was. I was an
honor student. I had two part-time jobs. I just made
one mistake."

Maybe it's because it's Lent, but I couldn't help
hearing the cry of the sinner in Allison's voice. "I just
made a mistake, God. Please forgive me. Please give
me Easter."

Luckily for all of us, God hears that plea with infinite mercy. Unfortunately for Allison, her father didn't.

"What did your father do when you told him you
were pregnant?"

There was a long pause. Allison searched her soul
for the words to describe the hurt. She hung her head....

"He told me to get out. He said as far as he was
concerned, I was dead.

"I said I was sorry. I really *am* sorry. I wish I could
start over again. That's what I keep thinking, Sister. I

wish I could roll back time to two years ago.

"I would do anything to get him to forgive me. Anything."

Just a few weeks ago, Allison gave birth to a beautiful baby boy. She's staying with us in our Mother and Child program and she's doing really well. She is proving to be a dedicated and loving mother.

She's really a gem.

But she's a gem without a home now. And I can't stop thinking about Easter when I see her.

Imagine if God treated us the way Allison's father treated her. Better yet, imagine if Allison's father treated her the way God treats us all.

He would have said to Allison, "Look. I know you made a mistake — a big one. And you know you made a mistake.

"So I'm going to give you 40 days to think about it and understand it, and try to do better.

"And at the end of it all, we'll rejoice. All will be forgiven."

Imagine if Allison's father had given her Lent ... and then Easter.

Allison made a whopper of a mistake, no doubt about it. She's going to be paying for that mistake the rest of her life. But the lost educational opportunities, the lost childhood, the overwhelming responsibilities of being a mother at age 16 ... all that is nothing compared to losing the love of her father.

That's the part that broke her heart.

Thank God — and you — we were here for her. We

have welcomed her and given her the chance to make up for her mistake the only way she can now: to be as good a mother as possible, and to continue her studies and get her high school diploma.

And we have forgiven her. Thanks to you, we have given her the Easter forgiveness she deserves.

None of us can live without that. We are all too flawed. We all make far too many mistakes. We all need, really need, forgiveness all the time.

And none of us can stand to lose the love of our Father in heaven. That's the part that breaks our hearts.

God knows this about us. That's why He gave us Easter.

On that first Easter morning 2,000 years ago, He took us all by the hand and said, "OK. The suffering is over. I can see that you're sorry and I forgive you. Now let's have a celebration. Let's have a new life!"

I get that feeling every Easter. The lilies, the brightly colored clothes, the singing ... everything says to me, "It's a new life!"

I want so badly for Allison to feel that. I want her to wake up tomorrow morning and know that she is forgiven and she can start again with a clean slate.

Allison feels as if her father has buried her in the tomb — and won't let her have an Easter resurrection.

I wish her father would give her that....

Unfortunately, he won't, or can't.

But God can and does. And He asks us to tell His kids that He forgives them. And even more, He wants us to show His kids that He forgives them. He wants us to bring Easter to them.

That, more than anything else, is why we're here.

This is the one place where kids like Allison can find the forgiveness and joy of Easter.

Maybe we should even change our name to "Easter House...."

Chapter 15

"My parents beat me.
I had to get away," he'll say.

In a few days, you and I will take the innkeeper test again.

Remember the innkeeper of Bethlehem? The one who sent Mary and Joseph to the stable?

Sometimes I wonder about him. Maybe he didn't like the way Mary and Joseph looked. They were probably dirty and disheveled from their journey. And he sent them to the stable.

Maybe they were strangers and didn't have any money and he didn't want to be bothered and he figured charity only goes so far ... and he sent them to the stable.

For whatever reason, the innkeeper rejected God's family — and the Baby Jesus was born in a cold and dark stable.

All I know is that every year at Christmas time, God gives the innkeeper — you and me — another chance.

He says to us, "You may not recognize Them, but I'm going to send my family to you again and see how you do this time."

So on Christmas Eve, when kids start to pour in here from all over — hungry, tired, lonely kids — you and I will get another chance to be His innkeepers on our earth....

I'll stand at the door and see a boy, dirty and disheveled. "I just got off the bus from Toledo," he'll tell me. "My parents beat me, I had to get away," he'll say. "I ... I'm alone ... I'm cold ... can I, could you let me stay with you," he'll say.

"Of course," I'll say. "Please come in. I'm glad you found us," I'll say (even though it will hurt to say that, because all the time I'll be wishing he was home, spending time with a family that loved him and wanted him). And that moment, I'll also see Joseph in that dirty, tired face.

Then a young girl, pregnant, will come to the door. "I made a mistake and got pregnant," she'll say. "My dad got so mad he beat me and I ran away. I've been on the street for months and I'm so tired. Please, please can I stay here tonight?" she'll ask.

"Please, come in," I'll say, as I hug her. "You're welcome here." And as I lead her inside, she will wipe away her tears and whisper a faint "thank you," too tired and too embarrassed to even look me in the eyes. At that moment, it will be easy to see Mary in that girl's face.

Late in the evening, a young man will come to the door. He won't be nice. He won't be cute.

He'll be hungry and cold and dirty and a little loud. He won't say where he came from or why he has no place to go on Christmas Eve. He'll just say no one wants him. No one likes him.

And he'll be right.

He'll say he's sick. He'll say he doesn't care what

happens to him ... he's going to die anyway.

He'll try to ruin everyone's Christmas Eve.

And that's when God will wink at me from heaven and say, "Thought this was going to be easy, Sister? Now do you feel like the innkeeper? Don't you want to send this kid out to the stable? Can you see my Son in his face? Can you? Really?

"You know, a lot of people didn't like my Son, either. Sure He was beautiful when He was a baby, but when He grew up He was considered a troublemaker. He was loud and He said things people didn't want to hear. He made them uncomfortable.

"He didn't have the right background. He knew He was going to die soon. That can give you a certain edge.

"My Son shared more with this kid than you want to admit.

"Look hard. He's there."

I'll look hard. Past the hurt. Past the attitude. Past the street-hardened eyes. Past the fear.

And I'll think I see Him. Somewhere past all the hurts of the world, I'll try to see Jesus. And I'll reach out and hug him (if he'll let me) and let him know how glad we are that he found us on Christmas Eve.

And at that moment, the wonderful miracle of Christmas will begin again at Covenant House.

Sometime during the night, those glittering lights over Times Square — the ones that say "Girls, girls, girls!" — will be transformed into the Star of Bethlehem.

Sometime during the night, all those sad, lonely

kids will feel new hope.

The kid from Toledo will wake up feeling wanted and loved for the first time in his life. The pregnant girl will feel safe and forgiven for the first time in her life.

Most of all, the angry kid — the one with Jesus in his eyes — will soften just a bit.

True, his life won't have been changed overnight. But when I look into his eyes on Christmas morning, I'll see something I wasn't able to see hours before — the faint but glimmering realization that "yes, there are people in this world who care about me ... there is hope ... maybe I too will have a chance for a better life."

And though that glimmer in his eyes will be faint, it will shine every bit as sure and as strong as that star that hung over Bethlehem 1,996 winters ago. It will be one of the most beautiful sights I've ever seen.

That's the miracle of Christmas at Covenant House....

Chapter 16

*"Every time I tried to ask any questions,
they told me to shut up or they'd kill me."*

"They put a gun to my head, Sister. They said they were going to kill me. I started crying. I thought I was dead."

The young boy sat erect in the chair in my office and tried not to look scared. Even from 10 feet away, I could see his body shaking, from his eyeballs down to his toes. Sitting there, wearing out his knees with his hands, he looked like a little boy who had just awakened from the worst nightmare of his life. As it turned out, he had....

"Who put a gun to your head, Steve?" I said. "Please back up a little bit for me."

"I guess they were drug dealers," he said. "I don't know who they were or why they grabbed me. They thought I was someone else.

"I live in Rhode Island, and this morning I was walking down the street and this car stopped and these three guys with ski masks jumped out and one put a gun to my head and told me to get in the car. I tried to ask what the heck was going on, but they just pushed me in the car.

"They blindfolded me and drove me to New York. Every time I tried to ask any questions, they told me to shut up or they'd kill me. Five hours in the car and they wouldn't even let me go to the bathroom.

"Then they took me to some big building. It sounded empty, like a warehouse or something. They said I ripped off a big drug dealer and I was going to pay for it. They were joking about all the different ways they'd kill me.

"All that time, they had a gun against my head. Every time the guy with the gun laughed, I was scared he'd pull the trigger.

"Finally, another guy walked in and he took one look at me and said, 'Hey. This is the wrong kid,' and he chewed out the guys who had grabbed me.

"But then I was afraid they'd kill me, anyway. You know, so I wouldn't talk. I'm just glad they blindfolded me first so I didn't see their faces. 'Cause if I did, I'm sure they would have killed me.

"But after kicking a few chairs and yelling a lot, the head guy said, 'Let the kid go.'

"We got back in the car and drove for a while, then they let me out. They told me to keep the blindfold on and count to 100.

"When I was done counting, they were gone.

"I was in an alley. I didn't know where I was. I didn't have any money. I didn't know what to do.

"I finally found a cop and he brought me to Covenant House. He said you'd help me. Can you help me get home?"

"Sure, Steve," I said. "We'll call your parents right away. Are you OK?"

"I guess so. Man, I was so scared. They were really going to kill me."

"It's OK now, Steve. You're safe now. We'll get you home as soon as we can, OK?"

"OK," he said. "You sure?" he said. "Thanks," he said.

Steve stayed with us last night, and took the first bus home this morning. (He kept looking back over his shoulder when I walked him over, afraid that someone might be sneaking up on him. I'm sure he never closed his eyes for a second on that bus, all the way home.)

His mother just called me a few minutes ago to tell us he was home and to thank us. I could hear Steve in the background, talking to her the whole time. "Tell Sister I said thanks again," he kept saying. "Make sure you tell her I said thanks." She was crying and could barely get the words out.

So I'll say it for her, and Steve. Thank you. Thank you for making sure Covenant House was there for a good and decent kid who was lost and penniless and terrified on the streets of New York and didn't have a clue what to do.

I wanted to tell you this happy ending story because we rarely see one that ends so simply. And I wanted to show you just how many ways a kid can end up alone and vulnerable on the streets of our big cities.

Most kids aren't kidnapped at gunpoint, but they are kidnapped in different ways. They are driven out of their homes by abuse and dropped into the waiting arms of a sex and drug industry that puts a different gun to their heads.

Steve escaped them, thanks to you (make no mistake about it — if he had been alone on the street just 24 more hours, they would have found him, and begun to devour him). A lot of our other kids, way, way, way too many, won't be so lucky.

Epilogue

Thank you for taking the time to read this book. I know it hasn't been easy reading.

Shocking tales about children can be painful, even overwhelming.

When I was asked to take over the running of Covenant House, I was at the age when many Americans retire. While members of religious orders never really retire in the usual, kick-back-your-heels sense — I still thought it was time to slow down. Not to speed up!

And the thought of dealing with hundreds of hurting, street-hardened, mistrustful kids day after day was painful — even overwhelming.

So I said no.

The Covenant House Board of Directors kept after me. After they asked a fourth time, I finally gave in — while still thinking, "God, what are you doing? Why *ME*?!"

Since then, God has proven that He was right. There are days when this job is incredibly painful, even overwhelming. But each day, along with chilling tales of horror, come some of the most beautiful, heroic, faith-inspiring stories I've ever heard.

I've tried to share some of these feelings with you on these pages. I hope they've moved you as much as they've moved me.

And I hope they'll inspire you to join Covenant House by supporting our mission to save God's kids.

Above everything else, I have come to accept (and draw inspiration from) the certain knowledge that my days at Covenant House have been part of God's plan. I believe this with all my heart, that there are no accidents in the planning of our lives. What we do on this earth, what we become, is all part of a plan God has made for us. In a very real and profound sense, my time here has been a calling from God — something for Him.

Seven years later, I'm grateful that God insisted on bringing me here. I consider it the greatest, most profound blessing of my life.

*"I bound myself by oath,
I made a covenant with you ...
and you became mine."*

Ezekiel 16:8

*(Our oath, the first thing kids see
when they walk into our shelter.)*

Faith Into Action

Your invitation to join the
Covenant House Faith Community

By now you know that Covenant House is more than a shelter for kids — it's a mission inspired by, led by and dedicated to God. For some very special people, just reading about our kids is not enough. They want to be part of this work, to see and feel first hand what our kids go through.

It's for these people that the Covenant House Faith Community was created.

Our Faith Community is a group of full-time volunteers who put their faith into action by dedicating 13 months of their lives to the mission of Covenant House. These extraordinary people come from all walks of life, from every corner of the country. They are as young as 21 and as old as their mid-70s. But as different as they are, they all share a common purpose — to make our kids' world, and all our worlds, a better place than they found it. Community members live together in prayer and service to God and to the kids of Covenant House. Faith Community volunteers combine a faith-motivated giving of themselves with a deep commitment to serving Covenant House kids.

This commitment to adolescents and young adults

who are homeless is a true expression of the gospel and
an enriching experience for members of the Faith
Community. A life combining prayer and community
life becomes a support to the service commitment and
an opportunity to reflect and grow spiritually and per-
sonally. If you are over 21 years old, please consider
joining this special group of people.

*"Up until last year I was a perfectly normal gradu-
ate student, getting my Ph.D. and studying urban
poverty ... now I work with girls who were pregnant at
16 and kids my little brother's age who sold and used
drugs while my brother was still running a paper
route," says Ann, a Faith Community member. She
adds, "I come home so exhausted, I cannot see straight
... it's been the best year of my life."*

Please read on as two more Faith Community volunteers share their stories....

Missy

"I know it sounds corny," says Missy, *"but I
believe it was my destiny to come to Covenant House."*

"I first heard about Covenant House when my high
school youth group (from Whitehall, PA) came for a
tour in my freshman year. The tour of Covenant House
gave me the idea of becoming a social worker. As the
years went by, I received fund-raising letters from
Covenant House and majored in Social Work at Ohio
State University. In my senior year, I read about the
Faith Community at Covenant House in *Choices* (a
booklet about full-time volunteer opportunities). I

came for the Orientation — and I knew I had to join.

"I came to New York in September of 1995, to join a community I wasn't even sure I would fit into. My experience started with Formation, an extensive three-week program of workshops and sessions. I was suddenly spending all my time looking at myself. Where was I with my faith? How did I deal with others? How would I handle hostility or rejection from the kids? Was I up to loving and living in a community? How would I live a simple life, chastely, and with little money?

"I was making a commitment to pray daily with people I didn't know. I was making a commitment, I realized later, to love unconditionally. It was overwhelming — the first three weeks of non-stop self-examination. And in the back of my mind was the fear, 'Would I be able to work with the Covenant House kids?'

"When Formation was over, I was ready to get to work. I wanted to work in the Community program, a Covenant House storefront, which brings education and vocation services to the neighborhood. I liked it because such programs, it seemed to me, could keep kids where they lived and prevent them from ever having to go to the crisis center.

"My first job at Covenant House was as a Resident Advisor in the crisis center, working with our young girls. There are about 35–40 young women at any given time. When I interviewed for the position (yes, even though I was a volunteer, I had to interview like any other staff member would), I was asked the exact question I had been asking myself during the three weeks of Formation: 'What makes you think you can do this kind of work?' 'I don't know,' I said. 'I only know I want to learn.'

"For the first few weeks I spent most of my time observing. Gradually, I began to get a case load. I was assigned as a Counselor to new kids as they came in. It was difficult at first because I was intimidated by the rough exterior the kids sometimes have (it's a defense mechanism by kids who have been hurt so often they can't trust anyone). What was really hard for me was to be direct and to put myself in a position where I might have to say no. I didn't know what would happen if I did. I was afraid.

"Naturally, I am not very assertive. I am a nice person who wants others to be nice, too. But with the encouragement of my supervisor, I began to take risks. I began to get 'in their faces.' To say yes, no. To set limits and to hold them. At the same time I was growing more confident, I also developed a sense of humor and an ability to joke around which helped me (and I think the kids) enormously.

"Working at the crisis center turned out to be a very good testing ground because of the intensity and the diversity of the staff and residents. I got stretched and challenged constantly.

"It was the first Christmas I ever spent away from my family. I dreaded it. However, it turned out to be the best Christmas I ever had. We started out with a prayer service, a wonderful breakfast and then the kids opened presents. For many, it was the first Christmas where they got attention. Many couldn't believe how many gifts they received, and how nice the gifts were. 'This is the best Christmas of my life, and I have never received so many gifts,' they all said. One kid gave all the stuff she had to some other homeless people who gather on 41st St. I was amazed.

"After eight months at the crisis center, I had the opportunity to go to work at the Community Center. At the end of my year, there was an open position and I was hired as a Caseworker. No matter who walks in our doors, we help them, either directly, or with a referral.

"While there were many challenges and growing pains in the work with the kids, I found the Faith Community to be very supportive. I was very fortunate to be able to come to eight other community members and share experiences. Many days I was frustrated and exhausted. Other days I had joys to share, and I could be supportive of others. The work changed me; the Community supported me. I made dear friends. And I fell in love with New York.

"Did I make a difference? Yes. Yes, I believe I did. I started off the year anxious to help, but then I discovered that it wasn't my doing or my helping, but simply my being present. Just being there, that is the doing."

Sally
"I feel something I never felt before."

"I've been in the Covenant House Faith Community for two months. Why didn't I do this 20 years ago? It feels like exactly what I should be doing.

"For 12 years I worked my way up the ladder in the advertising profession. As a Marketing Manager, I found myself pretty much at the top of my specialty and grew bored with it. More money could be made. I could be a Vice President. I could tell more people what to do. But the creative part, the brainstorming, was missing. The higher you go, the less that kind of creativity is part of your job. I had been away from the Church, too. Something was definitely missing in my life.

"I found myself reaffirming my spiritual values, including living the gospel. A Jesuit led me to explore the gospel, which forced me to look at my lifestyle. I could not ignore something that said I needed to look beyond my own door. On a retreat at a monastery, Sister Mary Rose's *Are You Out There, God?* book appealed to me. When I asked about the volunteer program, I told myself I was just curious. Then I found myself coming to New York for an orientation. The Director of the Faith Community was very supportive. It seemed that slowly but deliberately, I was being led to a major change.

"I struggled for a year with my own unwillingness to volunteer. It meant going into a totally new situation, leaving the comfort of my income, my house, my friends. Working through my own inertia was a long process, but a force had been set in motion that I knew couldn't be denied.

"Now that I'm here, I feel something I never felt before, even at the most exciting moments of working in the advertising world, which is a sense of peace and a sense of integration. I'm in touch with a deeper part of myself. I'm doing what my heart has led me to do, rather than putting it off for later. I have a sense of being a whole person, even though I'm sometimes overwhelmed.

"Recently I spent a day agonizing about this kid Joe who might have to go back to Rikers (a New York City prison) because he was suspended from Covenant House for fighting. I found myself thinking, 'I can't deal with this kid's pain,' but somehow I was dealing with it. How is that you can be happy, at peace and disturbed at the same time? I don't know. But it all happens together, and it's a different way of living. I think I'm hooked!

"I get more than I give because these kids are incredibly strong — what they've been through is unbelievable and the fact that they're still functioning is remarkable. Joe's mother died in his arms of asthma when he was 12 years old, and he lived on the street since then selling drugs. I'm surprised he didn't go completely out of his mind.

"Joe had a court date last week. I wrote a letter to the court on his behalf, and they agreed to give him another chance. He's staying with his sister during his 30-day suspension from Covenant House and contin-ues to come to classes and workshops here each day.

After a month, he can come back into Covenant House, and we can tell the court that we're doing OK. They were wonderfully cooperative.

"This experience is part of my own healing. When the love comes through, it heals not only who we work with, but it heals me, in ways that I don't need to understand. Today I felt really happy. I didn't have any reason to feel happy. We started singing songs with this one kid on the elevator and just felt this joy. There was no reason for it.

"In the Faith Community, we live a three-part commitment — prayer, whatever our connection to God is, community and service. That's the commitment we make for 13 months. When you know other people who have made that commitment, that knowledge is very supportive. We pray together morning and evening. Wednesday nights we have dinner, a meeting and Mass together. We care about each other. I was concerned that I wouldn't find things in common with much younger people, but that's not been true at all. There's also someone in Community now who's 75 years old.

"I have many good friends back in California, but this is on a new level. I didn't choose any of these people, but I couldn't have made a better choice, which is really kind of strange....

"From the giving you receive."

Where do we go from here?

My newsletters tell an incredible story ... but they only tell part of the story. Wrapped around the letters I wrote to my friends, I've also included words written to me by others — poems and prayers written by our kids, and letters sent to me by donors who were moved by what they see happening in America today.

And almost every word in this book — whether they were penned by me, a runaway kid, a nervous grandmother, or a teenager in school — carries a consistent message: the American family is falling apart. And we must, each of us, do what we can to repair it. Now!

I passionately believe the breakdown of the family unit is the single deepest ethical and moral challenge of our generation. Whether we respond to it will depend on the resolve and willingness of all of us to commit ourselves to the care and protection of family life. The time for repairing endangered families and rescuing their children is not after they have fallen apart!

The question then is ... how? How can each of us make a difference in repairing the American family? And how can we begin to make that difference now?

Because the survival of the family is so very important to our futures, we have prepared a special Family Survival Guide which can be found on the following pages. This Guide features the best things we've learned over the years working with hundreds of thousands of kids, as well as good, time-tested values that we never let ourselves forget. We hope you will share these pages with a parent you know who may need help. Thank you!

Family
Survival
Guide

Reflections on
Raising Kids Today

Values – Teaching Them in Today's World.

Communicating your values has never been more important than it is today. And the good news is, it all begins and ends with you.

When all is said and done, parents have far more influence over instilling values in their kids than any other factor.

Here are some simple, and very important, things we should all remember about values, and passing them along:

- Kids get their sense of what's right and wrong from people they love and respect. No one has more influence over teaching values than you do. Your input can make all the difference!

- When it comes to teaching values .... action *always* speaks louder than words. Kids today have a "show me" mentality. They need to see the values lived out by you. Respect for life, respect for other people, honesty, integrity ... kids get those from watching you. The old saw has never been more true ... children *do* learn what they live!

- Families are still the best vehicle for raising children. A loving, nurturing family unit, of whatever form, creates the kind of environment kids need to learn what's right and wrong ... and how to love themselves too. Values are best inculcated in an environment of love and acceptance.

- Always take time to sit and talk to your kids. Don't be afraid to say what you feel (but don't ever be too closed to listen to what your kids think).

- Always strive to teach your kids to love and respect themselves as children of God. A healthy love and respect for themselves is incredibly important for any kid. It's also the first essential step in helping a kid also learn a love and respect for those around him, and God.

- Nobody has said it better than Jesus. Those three words, "Love Thy Neighbor...." are an important message for every kid!

You've Got a Tough Job.

Most of us were never taught to be parents. So we can't help but disappoint ourselves sometimes. How often have you heard yourself using the very words you hated hearing from your own parents?

And when our kids become teenagers, it gets even harder. They seem to reject everything we've taught them. As far as they're concerned, we know nothing. Our values and beliefs are constantly challenged. Every word we utter is seen as interference. Emotions run high.

But we're more important to our teens than ever. As they try out the values of their peers, who are more influential than ever, we counter the pull of drugs and alcohol. These entangle children every day and can ruin their lives.

The Stakes Are High.

Teenagers who don't get what they need at home look elsewhere. Some run away from home. Many more consider other ways of running from pressure — a once bright and happy son escapes to drugs, a vivacious daughter starts drinking. Think about these facts:

- Each year, one million students drop out of high school or are chronically truant.
- Four out of 10 teenage girls will become pregnant before age 20.
- Although marijuana use has declined in the past years, addiction to cocaine, especially crack, has doubled.
- One in four teens develops a drinking problem during his teen years; about 10,000 will die in alcohol-related accidents this year.
- Each year, 5,000 to 6,000 teens die in suicide-related deaths, and the number is growing, one every 90 minutes. For every death, at least 100 other young people attempt suicide.

The Turbulent Teens.

Teens face many pressures that adults don't take seriously. Their bodies are changing — they have to adjust to the new person they see in the mirror. They feel different. They become interested in sex.

Self-doubt is constant. They feel pressure to conform and fear ridicule if they don't.

These changes can be bewildering, frightening and even depressing.

Teens can have remarkable insights. But they also surprise us with their lack of good judgment.

Your Teen Needs You.

At the time teenagers are crying out to be treated as adults, they also need a nurturing home, a refuge. And though they deny it passionately, they need structure, limits, lots of help sorting out their lives and most important, love.

In the turbulence of growing up, it is important for us parents to remember (even if our teens seem to forget) that we love each other. In the end, that's what makes the whole struggle worthwhile.

How Well Do You Know Your Kids?

You may say, "My teenager wouldn't do that." Most don't. But even if yours wouldn't, think about the following questions:

- Where is your child right now?
- What are your teen's deepest fears?
- Who is your son or daughter's best friend?
- Do your teen's friends feel welcome in your home?

Remember, a strong relationship with your children is the best way for you to guide them, and to prevent them from becoming a sorry statistic.

Getting Along With Your Teen.

Here are some ideas and techniques you can try to improve your relationship with your teen. If they don't work at first, keep trying. They take practice.

1. Make time for your teen. Find an activity you enjoy doing together and pursue it. If your invitations are declined, keep asking.

2. Listen, really listen. Because parents have so much to do and so little time, we often try to listen while cleaning, washing dishes or fixing the car. Put your chores aside so your teen knows you're really paying attention.

3. Take the long view. Don't treat minor mishaps as major catastrophes. Choose the important issues. Don't make your home a battleground.

4. Tolerate differences. View your teenager as an individual distinct from you. This doesn't mean you can't state your opinion if you disagree.

5. Respect your teenager's privacy. If a behavior is worrying you, speak up.

6. Let your teens sort things out themselves. Never say that you know how your teen feels. They believe their feelings (so new and personal) are unique. They'll learn otherwise — without your help. And never imply that their feelings don't matter or will change. Because teens live in the present, it doesn't matter that they'll soon feel differently.

7. Don't judge. State facts instead of opinions when

you praise or criticize. Stating facts like "Your poem made me smile," or "This report card is all Cs and Ds!" leaves it up to your teen to draw the appropriate conclusions. Teens are sensitive about being judged — positively as well as negatively.

8. **Be generous with praise.** Praise your child's efforts, not just accomplishments. And don't comment on the person. "You're a great artist" is hard to live up to. "I loved that drawing" is a fact and comes from your heart.

9. **Set reasonable limits.** Teens need them. Your rules should be consistently applied — and rooted in your deepest beliefs and values.

10. Teach your teen to make sensible decisions and choices by encouraging independence and letting your teenager make mistakes. Don't step in unless you have to.

How to Make Anger Work.

All parents get furious at their children. We can't help it. But some parents feel bad about being angry and keep quiet. Though it's easy to say things in anger that you don't mean, anger can also spark talks that will help you and your teen get to know each other better.

Some Guidelines.

• When you get mad, don't blame or accuse. Say how you *feel* — annoyed, irritated, upset, etc. —

and why. Be specific. Talk facts. Blaming only forces a teen to argue his point, arouses tempers, and kills dialogue.

- Think solution, not victory. Don't try to win arguments.

- Stick to the present incident. Fighting old battles will only aggravate a situation.

- Be careful not to attack your teen's person or character. Say, "I'm furious that you didn't clean up after the mess you made" — *not*, "You're a lazy slob!" Your son or daughter may give up trying to improve.

- If the situation is touchy, put your ideas in a letter. You can say exactly what you mean — and your teen will have time to think it over before answering.

Signs That Your Child Needs Outside Help.

- Suicidal talk of any kind. A suicidal teen may also give away valued possessions, make a will, talk about death or dying or say his family would be better off without him.

- Recent changes in sleeping or eating habits, thinking patterns, personality, friendships, study habits, activities. A sudden unexplained end to a long depression often precedes a suicide attempt. Major weight loss can be a sign of bulimia or anorexia — dangerous problems.

- Drug or alcohol use. You might notice: irrational

or irresponsible behavior, lying, secretiveness, severe mood swings, a sudden increase in accidents. A teen with a problem may have dilated pupils or wear sunglasses indoors, or complain about not sleeping or not feeling well. Valuables may disappear. You may find drug paraphernalia or alcohol containers around the house.

- A recent change in friends who you feel may be involved with drugs or alcohol may indicate that your child is involved or be a sign that your child is having other problems.

- Law-breaking behavior, even if the police and courts aren't involved. You might notice new possessions and money not accounted for.

- Poor self-image. Doubts are normal. But persistently low self-esteem is a problem.

- Serious depression. Listlessness, loneliness, withdrawal, difficulty making friends.

- Rebelliousness to the point of total, continual defiance.

- Problems at school, including class-cutting, absenteeism, a sudden drop in grades.

- Fears or anxieties that interfere with everyday activities.

- Problems between family members that aren't solved by listening and discussing. In fact, family changes such as a death, divorce or remarriage are times when teens often need some outside help.

When to Get Help For Yourself.

- Things aren't going well with your family but you can't figure out why.
- You disagree totally with positions your spouse has taken on issues concerning your teen and the two of you can't find a compromise.
- You have trouble holding a job.
- You are abusing drugs or alcohol.
- You get violent with your teenager and can't control yourself.
- Your spouse gets violent with you or your child.

What to Do If Your Teen Runs Away.

Most kids who run away return within 48 hours. Those who stay away can find themselves in many dangerous situations. So do everything you can to bring your child home.

- Keep a notebook recording steps you've taken and dates.
- Check in with: neighbors, relatives, and your teen's friends, teachers, employer or co-workers.
- Contact local hangouts and hospitals.
- Call the police. Have an officer come to your house to take a report and pick up recent photos, dental records and fingerprints if available. Get his name; badge number and phone number; the police report number; and the name of the officer who will follow up.
- Make sure the police lists your teen in the National

Crime Information Center (NCIC) to the state clearinghouse on missing children, if there is one in your state.

- Contact the National Center for Missing and Exploited Children for help with law enforcement officials — 1-800-843-5678.
- Call the Covenant House NINELINE for support and to check for messages. Leave a message. Also check with any local runaway hotlines.
- Contact runaway shelters locally and in nearby states.
- Make posters with photos of your teen, listing: age, height, weight, hair and eye color, complexion, physical characteristics (such as scars, birthmarks, braces or pierced ears), circumstances of disappearance, your phone number and police contacts. Distribute these to truck stops, youth-oriented businesses, hospitals, law-enforcement agencies.
- Be prepared for the first conversation with your teen. Whether in person or by phone, show concern, not anger. Say, "I love you."
- Prepare to quickly begin resolving the problems which caused your child to leave home. When your child returns home, emotions are likely to run high. Someone outside your family can help you all deal with these emotions. You may find that planned time for your teen in a temporary residence or shelter is necessary while you are resolving problems. So get outside help from a trained counselor.

Need expert help or support?

Call our NINELINE counselors at 1-800-999-9999.

We'll put you in touch with people who can help you right in your hometown.

1-800-999-9999

This call is free.

Covenant House
346 West 17th Street
New York, NY 10011-5002

Covenant House New Jersey
Atlantic City:
3529 Pacific Avenue
Atlantic City, NJ 08401

Newark:
14 William Street
Newark, NJ 07102

Covenant House Washington
3400 Martin Luther King, Jr. Ave., S.E.
Washington, D.C. 20032

Covenant House Florida
Fort Lauderdale:
733 Breakers Avenue
Fort Lauderdale, FL 33304-4196

Orlando:
888 N. Orange Avenue
Orlando, FL 32801

Covenant House New Orleans
611 North Rampart Street
New Orleans, LA 70112-3540

Covenant House Alaska
609 F Street
Anchorage, AK 99501-3596

Covenant House California
1325 N. Western Avenue
Hollywood, CA 90027-5611

Covenant House Texas
1111 Lovett Boulevard
Houston, TX 77006-3898

Covenant House Michigan
4151 Seminole St.
Detroit, MI 48214

Covenant House Canada
20 Gerrard Street East
Toronto, Canada M5B2P3

Covenant House Mexico
Paseo de la Reforma 111
Mexico DF 06300, Mexico

Covenant House Guatemala
3a Avenida 11-28, 5to piso
Zona 1
Guatemala City, Guatemala

Covenant House Honduras
Apartado 2401
Tegucigalpa, D.C., Honduras

Covenant House Donor Assistance Line: 1-800-388-3888
Visit our website at: http://www.CovenantHouse.org

Please Help Me, God

Covenant House depends almost entirely on gifts from friends like you to help 44,000 homeless and runaway children every year. We provide food, clothing, shelter, medical attention, educational and vocational training and counseling to kids with no place to go for help. Please help if you can.

YES! I want to help the kids at Covenant House. Here is my gift of: ☐ $10 ☐ $20 ☐ $25 ☐ Other

Name _____

Address _____

City _____State _____ Zip_____

Please make your check payable to Covenant House.
Your gift is tax deductible.

☐ *Please send me your financial information.*

☐ Please send me _____ copies
of *Please Help Me, God.*

Many people like to charge their gift. If you would like to, please fill out the information below:
I prefer to charge my: ☐ MasterCard ☐ Discover ☐ Visa

Account # _____

Amount_____ Exp. Date _____

Signature_____

      Mail to: Covenant House
                  JAF Box 2973
                  New York, NY 10116-2973

Or, call 1-800-388-3888 to charge your gift on your
MasterCard, Discover or Visa.
                                  COUPON

Just a reminder....
Many companies match their employees' charitable donations. Please check with your company or your spouse's company. It could mean extra help for our kids.

Covenant House is a member of America's Charities, a nonprofit federation that represents a variety of national charities in workplace giving campaigns. To find out if your employer is a part of America's Charities call us at: (800) 458-9505.